T0365360

THEODORE M. WANDZILAK, M.D.

THE EAST DECK

Motel AND

SELECTED *Poetry*

Print information available on the last page

Rev. date: 04/23/2016

To order additional copies of this book, contact:
Xlibris
1-888-795-4274
www.Xlibris.com
Orders@Xlibris.com

Contents

Preface

As a chemistry major at Adelphi University in the early 1970s, I took a single course in beat poetry as a diversion from my major. Since that time, I became hooked on this genre of poetry. Perhaps it was because chemistry was so exacting and precise and beat poetry was just the opposite, often not adhering to standard syntax and punctuation. It seemed to produce a good balance in my life.

I was attracted to beat poetry for many reasons. Garrison Keillor, in his book *Good Poems*, described some of the principles of what he felt good poetry should entail. Keillor stated, "Good poems tend to incorporate some story, some cadence or shadow of story." Keillor quoted Charles Bukowski: "There is nothing wrong with poetry that is entertaining and easy to understand. Genius could be the ability to say a profound thing in a simple way." It seemed to me that beat poetry, for the most part, did tell a story and that it was entertaining and easy to understand.

Many times when I read beat poetry, it became apparent to me that the poet was spilling out complex emotions on the page in simple words. Often I felt that through a story of everyday circumstance, something profound was said. I found myself saying why did I never think of life like this before? I found myself crying, laughing, or in deep thought over a simply written poem.

Good work in many avenues of life often comes from passion. The beat poet Lawrence Ferlinghetti said, "For great poetry to be born, there must be hunger and passion." So through hunger and passion, a story is told in simple language with profound implications.

I hold the above tenants of poetry close to my heart in this collection of poems written over the past forty years.

The East Deck Motel, located in Montauk, New York, was built in the 1950s. Adjacent to Ditch Plains Beach, it was a mecca for surfers, fishermen, and beach lovers for over fifty years. The motel was recently sold, and efforts by the Town of East Hampton failed to acquire the property. What will become of this endeared property remains undetermined as of 2015.

Photograph of the East Deck Motel by Theodore M. Wandzilak, November 2001.

To my daughter

Lara Jane

For without her help,
this book would not be possible.

I have slept in a hundred islands
where books were trees.
. . . .
I have dwelt in a hundred cities
where trees were books . . . .

—Lawrence Ferlinghetti

Never Spoke

I died in my mother's chair,
Where she chain-smoked.
I died her death of endless neglect.
As she watched white walls turn to tar-stained yoke,
she never spoke.

I died in my father's chair,
Across from my mother's.
I died his death of endless regret.
As he watched white walls turn to tar-stained yoke,
he never spoke.

I died in my ancestral chair,
Where I drank red wine.
I died a death of endless despair.
As I watched white walls turn to carmine,
we never spoke.

Quiet

In my empty new home, I had an empty courtyard.
In the brick courtyard,
I listened to the quiet.

With my eyes closed,
Something strange happened.

I heard the distant call of a crow.
A gentle breeze wandered through the leaves of a nearby tree.
I heard the faint cry of a child and the sound of a bouncing ball.

Then a train's whistle was barely audible,
And I heard the beat of a heart pounding louder and louder.

Yes, in the quiet of my courtyard,
The sounds became deafening.

Sometimes it is so quiet you cannot hear a thing,
And sometimes it is so quiet you hear everything.

Seven Years Later

Waterfall splashing
Westminster chimes clanging

Distant sounds beyond the courtyard
Now gone

Come back to me, my beyond!
Come back to me, my beloved beyond!

Inside the brick courtyard
I had created a prison for my ears

Midnight in Moscow

Near midnight,
The Bolshoi Ballet,
Maya Plisetskaya,
I saw her dance.
Perplexed by
Her incomprehensible mystery.

It was midnight of her life,
And the Russians buried her in red roses
Upon the stage she alone owned.
This prima ballerina
Drowned in the warm red blood of these roses.
Her figure,
A white candlestick,
Melted in this hot blood
As all of Moscow cried moist waxed tears.

Melancholia

I was twenty in St. Petersburg
Walking down a path of mass graves on either side

Shostakovich's Seventh Symphony
Softly whispered through the icy air
From the bronze statue of Mother Russia

Five hundred thousand Russians or more
Men, women, children, soldiers under the granite slabs
Most died of starvation
In the German blockade of the city

I was twenty
People that I never knew dying a gruesome death of starvation

The city never surrendered
The enormous endurance of people dying for a cause and pride
Inconceivable

I was twenty and too young to walk down this path

A Partial Autobiography

I was born with a remnant third nipple
I did not know what that meant for me

When I swam in salt water
At Oyster Bay
Theodore Roosevelt watched over me

When I was eighteen, I drove a blue
'66 Mustang Sedan
I lived a good life then, on the sea and on the sand
And hoped my number did not come up in Vietnam

I cooked hot dogs at the Montauk Country Club
I didn't know my time was up

I saw Yul Brynner play *The King and I*
Before he died

Amazed I prayed
Never deprive me of my sight

I saw Stan Getz play at the
The Blue Note Club
The Magic Marvel
I lost my ticket stub
I have seen a half-moon lay on its side
Above a bright Hawaiian sky
I rode the canoe moon through the night
Amazed I prayed
Never deprive me of this flight

I have seen the unicorns at the Cloisters
And I wanted to take one home with me

I have walked on the frozen river Neva
The ice fisherman gave me a nasty fever

I caught a wahoo in Turks and Caicos
The sharks left the head and ate the carcass

In Monte Carlo I saw the aquarium of Jacques Cousteau
And at the Hôtel de Paris
Devoured a chocolate gâteau

I have dissected the organs of a cadaver
The liver, lungs, and gallbladder

I have cut the eyes out of a dead man
In a cold dark morgue
And served them up as a Persian king's smorgasbord!

Then I thought
Never deprive me of this culinary delight

I have been to Der Kölner Dom
And drank Rhine wine from the Hessen
Therein my genitals were permanently
Covered with Cologne 154 essence!

I have burst forth from the wall at Bloody Bay
Eighty feet under, I looked up and saw a spotted eagle ray!

I have delivered fourteen lives
Each followed by fourteen placentas
Therein, I found elation upon this earth,
Unequaled to a dinner of lobster polenta

I have a favorite road, you know,
In East Hampton called Dunemere Lane

A thousand times I've closed my eyes
And opened them again to peer on Dunemere Lane
Where the Maidstone Club leads to timeless
Hedges and foggy terrain

I have married and divorced
And married and divorced again. Please

Nevermore deliver me to this plight

For four years, I was unable to walk
So instead, I surfed by the light of the moon
My feet steadied only by my surfboard
When I could walk again
Each step was on a lotus flower with pride
And with each step I smiled wide
Nevermore deprive me of my stride

The East Deck Motel

There was a cool onshore wind that brought a whisking fog
That night to the decks and beach beyond the East Deck Motel

The whisking fog was kind of eerie, almost really scary
Vanishing into the black waves beyond the deck

Strolling near the shore
The fog filled my feet

I could barely tell land from sea
I knew where I was, but not exactly

Who knows the heart of a tear
But a tear itself?

We found a soft place to lie
Between the sand dunes and sea grass

Tobacco smoke mixed with fog
Caused a reverse rainbow of white-and-gray prisms

Here in the dunes we made love
And maybe, she was just pretending

Soon we made our way from the dunes
Back to the black beach

And then walking back to the break in the beach
Yes! Now the motel was in our reach!

As I stood on the salt worn planks
With a cold hand in mine
I felt like I was holding a cold clam in my hand
A shucked cherrystone clam!

Then I *knew* the heart of a tear
But I kind of knew it all along

The Springs

On a moonless summer night
We did fly on Springs Road without fright
One hundred miles per hour toward Fireplace Road
Our Mustang flashed
Only our headlights did show the path

So dark and narrow the road did seem
With fresh mint air flowing in a stream
And the trees with *Eyes in the Heat*
Seemed to stare upon us from everywhere

Here Jackson Pollock rode to a gravely death
A splash of red paint on gray cement

A crazy Corvette did pass us by
One hundred and twenty miles per hour it did fly

And only then was our mortality revealed
And yes, we were lucky to live
Where Jackson Pollock's
Shimmering Substance remained concealed

(The Springs, East Hampton, NY, 1973)

Fireplace Road

(September 1970)

Lion Head Rock Road
My girlfriend liked the name
Just before dawn, we went to Fireplace Road

At the inlet I caught a striped bass on a Rapala
We could see Gardiners's entire bay that day
And filled a bucket with littlenecks and cherrystones

For lunch we steamed the clams
Then downed them on the veranda
Each followed by a shot of Finlandia!

That evening we braised the bass in white wine
I asked her for a kiss
In the light of a canoe moon
In my blue '66 Mustang Sedan

The night wind was tender
She secretly hated striped bass
That September

Ditch Plains Trailer Park

Uncle Bud had a place in Montauk
At the Ditch Plains Trailer Park
Nothing ever seemed to bother him
A permanent smile, seemingly
He would say,
"You know, your entire outlook on the day
Changes when you have a beer at 11:00 a.m."

In the sixties, this was his weekend retreat
For fishing from Shagwong's Point to Lighthouse Point
And all the coves from Caswell's to Cavit's

Uncle Bud was an auto mechanic
Would carve and paint surface lures
When bottom-fishing he used spark plugs for sinkers

In the morning fog, I played Wiffle ball
A Giants fan—I imagined I was Juan Marichal
Body surfed at the beach and walked the cliffs
The years went by quickly

During my college days, I went to visit my uncle
I missed him and wanted to go fishing
He rigged up a pole for me with a spark plug sinker
And a bag of clams
He said,
"Walk down the beach until you reach
Warhol's cove."

Soon I had two blackfish
Uncle Bud filleted the fish
Panfried them with a little butter

To this day, the best—none other!

Uncle Bud was always happy to see me
With a genuine smile and greeting

It is true what they say
You will not be remembered by your material possessions
But by how you made people *feel*

Back in the sixties, the Trailer Park was kind of a tattered retreat
Now celebrities want to buy them for up for a million dollars each!

Young Love

I took her from Kentucky to New York
She wore a red velvet V cut and jeans
She did not know the proper way to use a knife and fork
We were in love in our day

From the island we took the train into Penn Station
We got lost in Times Square—too busy kissing on street corners
At the top of the World Trade Center, we were dizzy
We thought about having sex someplace in the city

Yes, we would go see a movie
Sit together in the back

La Derniere Femme—*The Last Woman*—sounded good
X-rated, perfect! A French porn film, all the better!
So we sat in the back, in the black
Not really paying too much attention to the movie

We were having fun in our seats
It was young love—listening to our hearts beat until . . .

Little by little scenes of nudity became constant
Why was the baby boy watching the adults anyway?

As we watched more of the movie, our hearts stopped beating
This was not porn—the movie had a plot and meaning!
We no longer could touch each other. We crossed our feet
Our hands now clenching our seats

Then blood squirted all over the screen
Gerard cut his member off with a knife!
The whole audience started to scream
We ran out into Times Square gasping for air

Soon our love was lost
But unlike old love, not at a great cost.

Distractions

Distractions are important in life
Hobbies are a good example of how to occupy your mind from . . .
You know what

A good distraction is watching sports
And even better becoming a sports fanatic

Work is another good one
Some people just work their whole life away

Because what if you had no distractions?
What if you had all the time in the world
To just sit there and think about . . .
You know what

If you had all the time in the world
To really face the hard, cold facts about life
You would be faced with the conclusion
That life is good and it is a miracle you are here

And who in the world
Could possibly stand so much happiness?
It would kill you! And now . . .
You know what

A lifetime of happiness! No man could bear it: it would be hell on earth.
—George Bernard Shaw

Zurich

When I was younger, I loved to be in the sun
Seasonal affective disorder
I feel so strung out under chocolate skies

So in winter months
I would go to tanning booths

I felt so good walking around town
And everyone saying, "You look so healthy."

When I was in Zurich
Swiss chocolate skies
Beautiful blondes walking around town with caramel tans
I thought Zurich must have a lot of tanning booths

Then I took the tram right through the clouds to the mountaintop
And there they were
All these beautiful blondes lying out in their bikinis
In crystalline alpine skies
Drinking coffee schnapps

And here I am back home
Going to tanning booths

Now I have squamous cell carcinoma on my ass!

The Exit

To die in your sleep
Well, that is no fun

An insidious death,
Like Alzheimer's
Your mind gone
My death will not be yours

I want the chance to think about it
I want to pick out my suit and tie
When I die
I always did look good in pastels

A little time to get ready
For the big show
Time to take that one last trip to St. Tropez
And get my last suntan

I want to look healthy when I die
Everyone peering at me in my casket
With my pastel suit and all suntanned
"Doesn't he look good!"

All my ex-wives and girlfriends saying:
"As handsome as ever! Well, he deserved it."

Time to think about my death
Existential matters
To come to no real conclusion why I lived or died

But at least
I want the *time* to come to that conclusion

Whatever Happened to Me

Whatever happened to me?
Green then, the forest full of leaves
Under the canopy
Patches of blue and white

The forest was peaceful then
Faraway trees swayed in the breeze
I imagined the sound of their touching branches
I was starting to learn the forest
And imagine nature's way

In the forest, I built a simple house
No address or mailbox or doorbell
I would lie in my hammock
And watch the raspberry sunset

I would return to another house before nightfall
Where there were worries in the walls
Where the television showed visions of world wars

Control in the forest
Red and black ant wars that I pitted
Pitted by bringing shovels full of these ants together
And watching them devour each other

In my home with the television
Television wars were the ant wars
Except that I had no control
Over shovels full
Of different people pitted together
Devouring each other

The television was never off in "the Big House"
The mailbox brought envelopes that no one wanted to open
Doorbells rang that no one wanted to answer
No, not peaceful forest
Just worries in the walls

Years passed by
I lost my imagination
I lost my vision of sounds

My house in the forest was still there somewhere
Now I lived in "the Big House"
With people wars on television
With doorbells I had to answer
With envelopes I had to open
No sunsets anymore

Whatever happened to me?

In Reverence of Lawrence Ferlinghetti

I am looking in the mirror this morning
And wondering if I should shave today

Does it really matter?
Will people really care if I shave some hair?

How did people shave before
They invented the Shick?

It's that time of month
My hormonal cycle

If I shave my legs
Maybe I will feel better
My partner feels better
When she shaves her legs

I am looking in the mirror this morning –
I see more than my physical self
I see that it is time for me to pack my bags

Elk

On a clear night with no moon
In a town called Bloomingtune
I ate elk with a runcible spoon!

After this carnivorous feast
I grew antlers and four hooves
Just like the mountainous beast
And trotted off in a puff
To see Yo Yo Ma
Haha!

His cello was sweet
It swept me off my hooves, not feet!
Later we fed Mr. Ma toasted farro
As he proceeded to eat my bone marrow!

A vampire cellist!
His Stradivarius so stellar
And a bloody good fella, indeed!

Bloomington, Indiana, 2013

A Raindrop

A summer storm with thunder sounded up high
Sending down millions of raindrops from the sky
Each raindrop is born up there somewhere
Exactly how and where, most people don't care

Perhaps the falling raindrops undergo reincarnation
Today it looks like it is raining meatballs

Do you think a raindrop really dies?
Or is it just recycled?

Maybe the inanimate comes back as the animate
Or vice versa
It's true—some days the rain comes down as cats and dogs

I believe my mother came back as an endless ringing telephone
In years past, I would not answer
Now that I am becoming closer to a falling raindrop
I miss her calls

The Stop Sign

Should I go out beyond the reef today?

I tried to save a life today
A last resort with an intravenous dopamine drip
In med school we called it "a no-hope-amine" drip
The patient died—I needed to take a trip

Like many times before
When I needed to get away
I left for the island of Kauai
And a place called Hanalei

From Hanalei I walked to where I had to go
I knew the place I had to reach
Past Lawai, I came to Ke'e Beach

The plumeria fragrance pranced along the shore
And asked me to dance once more
I could not accept
I could not take another step

My symptoms of Parkinson's were getting worse
I had watched my father die from this curse
And this is why I returned to Ke'e
Could I possibly die with dignity?

I have walked the path from Hanalei to Ke'e

Several times in my life

I have gazed out past the reef

Several times in my life

With a mind usually in turmoil and strife

No, I thought, I will go back to Hanalei

And think about the reef another day

Each time I looked out past the reef

I visualized a *stop* sign

And each time I lived another day

Yes, there is "hope-I-mean," in Hanalei

Do you want to go out past the reef today?

Perhaps you want to jump off the Sunshine Skyway Bridge in Tampa Bay?

We all have our own Hanalei or Tampa Bay

But will we all see the STOP sign

And turn away?

Some of us receive a moving violation

A Routine

Before I enter my office,
I always stop and look at the cemetery
Across the street.
Today there is a fresh grave being prepared.

Each morning I turn the light on
One by one.
I get my schedule for the day,
And place three pens in the
Left breast pocket of my lab coat.

Before I start my day, I try to remember
That life is not a race.
Slow down, I say. Watch your pace.

As the day goes on, I hug many people.
Sometimes I cry and laugh with my patients.

As I leave the office, I again
Glance to the cemetery.
The morning's fresh grave
Now holds Frank,
One of my dear patients.

A previous star running back at Notre Dame

He was just in the office last week.

Across the Room

Across the room in the examination chair,
Sat a lady with a blank stare.
Grown so old that her eyes forgot to blink.
She had not had a bath or washed within a week.
Now she could no longer think.

Years ago, she was vibrant and witty,
We talked so long about traveling to many a foreign city.

I say it is time to go, my dear.
I will see you back in one year.
Sullen-faced, white-faced, shrunken-faced.
At times past I would say,
"See you back in three months, my lady."
And we would laugh and hug
And dream of a new exotic city.

Now expressionless before me,
She said nothing as saliva dripped from her lips.

Grown old now and no longer firm and fair,
She sat motionless with that all too familiar stare.

I said to myself,
"Will that be me someday in the examination chair?"

Joe

Joe walks down my street
Sometimes he bypasses me
And takes the bus to Dairy Queen

Joe wears the same clothes every day
Summer or winter
Corduroy jacket and corduroy cap
And smokes his pipe all day
Cherry tobacco
Joe does not need cologne

Joe walks down my street
And sometimes comes into my office
Sits down for a rest
Or mostly comes in just to say,
"Hey, Doctor.
Is it okay if I just sit here a minute?"

Years ago I helped him see
Removed his cataracts by surgery

When I first met Joe
He said to me, "I don't know much about doctors,
Especially doctors who wear cuff links."

I met Joe for breakfast at Dairy Queen
I tried to tell him about people who wear cuff links

He just sat there. A grin would break out of nowhere
He looked at me with an abstract smile
A paranoid schizophrenic all the while

But he trusted me to help him see
And that's all that counts to me

Leo

Leo looked down upon the street below
People walked with a friendly glow
They walked and chatted

Leo looked down upon the street below
An ambulance flashed by
But Leo did not know why

A man walked his dog
On the street below
As snowflakes fell
And swirled around
All around the town below

Leo opened the curtain wide
Steel bars did partially hide
The whole world and not
Just the street below

Leo was now back in bed
He wanted to see the street below
He screamed, "Please let me see the Cyclades!"

The curtain was closed
The glass window turned to frost
As snowflake crystals
In his mouth were tossed

Snowflakes were now constellations
Twinkling behind closed eyes
In the universal darkness of his mind
Leo the Lion he did find

People

When I was young, I used to think
That people were just one big moving part
I did not look at people very closely
I just saw the forest and no individual trees
I did not know that people were made of different parts

I did not know the sum was the whole of its parts
I really did not know that the only part of a person
That made them different from another person
Is their mind
I can see the complexity of people now
Especially the complexity of the mind
And how the mind controls all parts
I see the *big picture* now
Because I see all the *little pictures*
Like putting the pieces of a puzzle together
And then all of a sudden, everything becomes clear!
No longer one big moving part
And I see the little trees that people are made of
All the trees that make people a forest

Insight

An apocalypse
Of shattered life looks me in the eye

In a dark night
The Ojo de Dios
A crucifix of color appears

In a triangle
The Eye of Providence
A Trinity of Christian theology
A possible salvation

The Evil Eye
Mauvais œil
Enchanting and bewitching

Only the apotropaic Eye of the Nazar
Can turn the Evil Eye to stone
The Eye of Horus
Is also a countervailing force

I wear the right eye of Horus Ra
In the sun
The falcon's left eye
Comforts me
Through night's long mystery

Paralyzed

I like to lie in bed at dawn
And watch the day develop

I like to hear the morning sounds
And smell the morning air

At daybreak
The steel sky knelt across my lanai

A sun-shower filled the air
A dense mist of pine and grass essence
The pindo palms beyond the lanai
Lie paralyzed in nature's presence

I like to lie in bed at dusk
And watch the day diminish

As darkness comes
I'm still in bed
You see
I made myself an invalid

A Somnambulant Voyage

I do not remember my birth
It was so long ago

I do not remember taking my first step
Although my parents have it on film somewhere

I barely remember anything about college
Except that I wanted to date a ballerina named Katrina
She would not date me because I studied chemistry

I remember just flashes of my dive trips to Bermuda
Like when the woman on her honeymoon
Got her ring finger chomped off by a barracuda

I have forgotten almost all of my life!
Where did it all go?
And whatever happened to my deceased wife?

Life is like a somnambulant voyage
Where only photographs remain alive in storage

But I know where *everything* is hiding
It's all in shoeboxes!

Betrayal

Looking toward the face of the mountains
I could see the summit in a clear California sky

Then at once, I had the feeling of betrayal
Gazing into the face of San Gabriel

I had a great day in Pasadena
Was San Gabriel really Mount Helena?

I visited the Huntington Estate
Gainsborough's Blue Boy did not know his fate
And I should have known mine

The same day I visited Pomona
The air was crisp and fresh all over
I felt that I was going to cry
At Saladong that night
We had a marvelous Pad Thai

After dinner I sat under fragrant tulip trees
The pink petals fell right next to me

Again I felt the feeling of betrayal
Gazing into the face of San Gabriel

All at once my body would not move
My eyes now locked on San Gabriel

Looking in the face of San Gabriel
I could now see the face of betrayal!

In a city thousands of miles away
She held a tulip-shaped ring in her hand
It was a pink diamond engagement band

I told her I was on business in Pasadena
But she found out
I was really sleeping with Leona from Pomona
In the face of San Gabriel, I saw my profile
I was really her betrayer!

London Fog

McManus and Wright played snooker all night
We watched the World Championship match
From our room in the Royal Horseguards Hotel

McManus hit a white into a red
And pocketed this red in a shot
All across the green snooker table bed

We watched each player score
From our room in the hotel
Room four fifty-four

Wright hit the white
He hit it right
Into the black
And into the end pocket it did smack

The time was five fifty-four
When we left for a drink at Harvey Nichols
At the bar were McManus and Wright
Having champagne, foie gras, and pickles

We then stopped by Sticky Fingers
For some fries and chicken fingers
And in the dense fog and dim light
Sat McManus and Wright
Using their cue sticks as chopsticks!

Yes, we were out late that night
When we returned to our hotel room
Room four fifty-four
Mcmanus and Wright were playing snooker all night
The time was nine fifty-four
And we watched each player score

McManus hit a white into a red
The exact same shot as before
All across the green snooker table bed

And Wright hit the white into the black
Into the same end pocket it did smack

The London fog was deep
Ah! Had we fallen into a deep sleep?
We never actually left the fourth floor
Room four fifty-four

In the morning outside our hotel room door
Stood a pair of snooker cues
Autographed by McManus and Wright
And a hand written note:
"Thank you for watching the match last night."

The Match

There were twenty people standing around the table
Watching the championship match.

I walked into the room with long blond hair,
Wearing shorts and Ditch Plains logo tee.
I had been surfing the past few days.

My opponent wore a black suit and tie.
His knowledge of the game was complete.
But as he took one look at me,
He did not look ready to compete.

I developed my pieces in an unusual way.
I disguised my attack.
Then Ditch Plains collided with Coco Beach.
He stopped leaning forward and sat back.

I played a game not in any book.
Frightened, he was on his heels and shook.
Observers started to ooh and aah.
My knight had pinned his queen and rook.

My opponent had a blank stare
In his permanent wheelchair.
Perhaps he deserved to win the match.
He was to be a physics major in college.

Alas! He had not yet learned what Einstein said,
"Imagination is more important than knowledge."

The Suffolk County High School Chess Championship
Bay Shore, Long Island, New York, May 1970.

La Bella Vita

I-75 down from Tampa

In the early evening there she would be in the front yard picking weeds.
At the age of eighty-seven, she would jump into my convertible like a Teenager.
What could she do if she had not smoked three packs a day since age 16?
She had good genes.

Many times I would have to take her to Walmart.
She reads the label of contents on every item bought.
She caressed every eggplant as if it were a newborn baby.
Three hours in Walmart! I thought I would have a stroke!

She had to try the samples in the deli department.
She said, "You have to taste the smoked turkey."
I just wanted to get the hell out of there!

Finally, after going through the endless checkout line,
She having to examine the price of every item on the receipt,
Match every penny for penny with her discount coupons,
My blood pressure was going through the roof.
Once outside, she lit up a cigarette cool and calmly.
There was no hurry in her life.

At home now, all the groceries are placed in their perfect living positions
Carefully and precisely.
I had to have a triple Johnny Walker Red on the rocks.
I was in a hurry to get home.
What exactly for, I did not know.

After the ordeal, she made the best
Eggplant parmesan I ever had!
This is how she showed her love for me.
She was eighty-seven. We called her "the Iron Lady."
Her weight was equal to her age.

Then she had to leave the house.
I would visit her at La Bella Vita.
When I entered the lobby, there was a gathering of people
All in wheelchairs forming a big circle—most were using nasal oxygen.
In the center of the circle was a hippie from the sixties,
His long hair tied back with a rubber band,
Doing a tai chi class
Saying, "You must breathe. You must breathe!"

When I entered the apartment, she was on the patio, smoking.
She hated the rule of no indoor smoking.
I sat on the couch. She sat by me.
Across from us, sitting in a remote-controlled recliner, was my father.
He had advanced Parkinson's disease and moderate Alzheimer's.
His new Exelon Patch was helping.

My mother asked me if I could take her food shopping at Publix.
I told her I was on a tight schedule.
I would go for her to pick up a few items.
Boy, did she hate this idea!
Why did I not take her?
Why was I in a hurry to do something else?

While at Publix, it dawned on me that everyone was ambulatory,

Going about their lives, strolling down the aisles.

A man walked up to the fruit section, peeled a banana, ate it, and

Walked right out the store.

I thought to myself, I should try doing the same someday.

Do I dare to eat a banana and not pay for it?

I had dinner with my parents. My mother was spoon-feeding my father.

After dinner, I went for a sunset walk on the beach.

There were people sitting in beach chairs watching the sunset, drinking beer.

There were couples strolling the shore, holding hands.

There were teenagers kissing, rolled up in blankets.

I pondered, did any of these people have any idea

What was going on at La Bella Vita? The good life!

Years Passing By

1998

Driving my daughter to school—the CD of Steely Dan
"Babylon Sisters"
She shook her index finger to the chorus:
"Tell me I'm the only one"

2006

The Hollywood Bowl—we saw Anti-Flag
Die for the Government
Jumping on the stage, they handed her drumsticks:
"Red, White, and Brainwashed"

2012

Spring Break in Siesta Key—CD played
"Cheeseburger in Paradise"
We sang in chorus:
"I like mine with lettuce and tomato"

2015

Louisville Cardinals Home Football Game:
Daft Punk
We sang the lyrics:
"We're up all night to get lucky"

Trout

My guide picked me up in Bozeman
We drove north toward Belgrade
North to the middle of nowhere
We parked by a small bridge
That spanned a branch of the Gallatin
We were going to walk upstream
Fish along the way

It was peak fishing season. We saw no one
Only the locals knew this place
Fishing this smaller stream was tough
The fly had to be presented quietly and naturally
He told me to mend my line gently

I looked around
In the distance stood the Bridger Range
The big blue Montana sky seemed endless
No one there but he and I
I smiled with my eyes

"Hoot owl" restrictions were in effect
Low water and high temperature
No fishing 2:00 p.m. till midnight
I watched him delicately handle the trout
"Now do not die on me"
As he filled their gills with oxygen
He respected life.

At 2:00 p.m. we had to go
Back at the bridge he told me
"Here the president fished"
I was proud of him!

No one there but he and I
I smiled with my eyes

Women vs. Men

Women want what they do not have;
Men have what they do not want.
Or
Men want what they do not have;
Women have what they do not want.

Printed in the United States
By Bookmasters